The Difficult Unicorn

A children's play

David Cregan

Samuel French — London
New York - Toronto - Hollywood

THE DIFFICULT UNICORN

First produced at the Southwark Playhouse, London, on 6th December 2002, with the following cast:

George Jackson	Brian Protheroe
Auntie Sharon	Darlene Johnson
Tracey	Carla du Bois
Mary Jackson	Deborah Farrington
Terry	Rhys McConnochie
Harry Jackson	Jonathan Peck
Stanley	Tim Preece

Directed by Jane Howell
Designed by Sophie Jump
Lighting by David Holmes
Sound by Rich Walsh
Choreographed by Geraldine Stephenson
Music by Brian Protheroe
Assistant director, Emma Bernard

COPYRIGHT INFORMATION

(See also page ii)

CHARACTERS

George Jackson, bank worker; middle-aged
Mary Jackson, George's wife, parking-meter attendant;
    middle-aged
Harry, George's son, office worker; aged twenty-one
Aunty Sharon, elderly but lively and made-up
Terry, Aunty Sharon's boyfriend
Stanley, a unicorn guardian, wears green baize apron
Tracey, works with Harry; aged twenty-one
The Unicorn
Mr Potter, line manager
Mr Scott, bank manager

The part of Mr Potter may be doubled with Terry and the
part of Mr Scott may be doubled with Stanley. The part of
the Unicorn is played by any two free actors but not
always the same actors.

SYNOPSIS OF SCENES

Time — the present

AUTHOR'S NOTE

The play is written so that it may, if desired, be performed with little more scenery than a table, some chairs, and a strip of petunias. The properties are rather more complex.

David Cregan

MUSIC NOTE

Optional incidental music composed by Brian Protheroe for the original production is available on request from the composer c/o Samuel French Ltd.

Other plays by David Cregan
with music by Brian Protheroe
published by Samuel French Ltd

Aladdin
Beauty and the Beast
Cinderella
Jack and the Beanstalk
Red Riding-hood
Sleeping Beauty

ACT I
SCENE 1

Elysian Fields

When the Lights come up, Stanley and the Unicorn are on stage. The Unicorn is operated by two actors and has a long golden horn. Stanley wears glasses, a green baize apron and carries a golden nosebag

Stanley (*to the audience*) Ah. This is what we call the Elysian Fields, which is a place where everything is very, very lovely. The very loveliest things of all are the unicorns who live here, of which this is a young example. (*To the Unicorn*) Show them how lovely you are, then. Frolic a bit.

The Unicorn frolics

(*To the audience*) See? Lovely as anything. And I'm Stanley, and it's my job to keep all their golden horns dusted and clean — twenty-four carat, yes — and to feed them Ambrosia, which is a sort of crunchy ice-cream, and I do it; don't I? Like this. (*He fits the golden nosebag to the Unicorn*)

The Unicorn eats hungrily

They could get it on their own from a crystal fountain, really, but they like it this way for the company. (*To the Unicorn*) Don't be so greedy, or you'll lose your figure. (*Intimately to the audience*) Actually, there's a bit of bother with this young person. He's not happy just being lovely. He wants to be useful, too, which is understandable but ridiculous. I've told him, you just stick to being beautiful, love, and thank your lucky stars you're not a cow. Leave being useful to those who know how to do it; pigs, sheep, things like that.

But it's no use, he won't be told, so what he's done, I'm afraid, what he's done is persuade me to set up this website for him on the internet, so that if anyone wants a bit of special help — heaven knows what sort — they just have to hit on unicornhelp@elysianfields.com, and we shrink down to nothing, and go buzzing off in little space capsules like hard-boiled eggs to do good work down there among all of you. Or we could if anyone knew about us, which fortunately no-one does. But there's always a first time, isn't there? And when it happens I honestly don't know how it'll turn out.

We'll have trouble finding the address for a start. And these little friskies can be so headstrong. (*To the Unicorn*) Finished? Right then, off we go for our morning prance-about, and hope no-one asks for anything too difficult. Come along, sweetheart, glitter away in the sunshine and be happy.

They exit

SCENE 2

The Jacksons' house, Peckham. Breakfast

George Jackson, middle-aged, and his son Harry, aged twenty-one, enter. They push on a table and some chairs. The table is laid with breakfast, including hard-boiled eggs and spoons

In the original production, the chairs remained on stage throughout the rest of the Act so that they could be rearranged as benches, office chairs, etc. where necessary

George and Harry sit at the table

George (*to the audience*) Aha, morning time in Peckham. A wonderful thing, morning time, especially today, (*to Harry*) eh, Harry?
Harry Dad — —
George (*to the audience*) My name is George Jackson; bank clerk. This is my breakfast, and I have a secret. It is this.
Harry Oh — —
George In a minute the postman will come and he will bring me two million pounds.
Harry Dad — —
George It will arrive here, at 19, Valley Road, Peckham, and it will be a wonderful surprise with which we will buy a swimming pool, a new car, and a well-manicured garden. We'll travel to Spain every other week, dance wildly into the night, invite our friends to meaty barbecues, shop at Harrods, drink sherry and be extremely happy. That is what is going to happen, and it is going to happen because I so much want it to happen that it will.
Harry Dad — —
George This is my son, Harry.
Harry This is my father, George, and — —
George (*to Harry*) Today, Harry, there is going to be two million pounds in the post. (*He cracks an egg and eats*)
Harry No, there isn't.

George Yes, there is, there is, there is! We're going to have leather furniture, and a shiny microwave and all sorts of glittering gadgets for the kitchen and — —

Harry You say this every day and it never happens.

George It will today.

Harry No.

George Yes.

Harry No.

George Yes.

Harry Dad, you're nuts! Lovely, but nuts!

George Harry, I'm your father, this is no way to speak to me, really. There will be two million — —

Harry You go on and on about it and it never, ever — —

George (*to the audience*) I am his father and there will be two million — —

Harry (*raising his voice*) There will not!

George (*to Harry*) I don't shout at you, so I don't think you should shout at me. I want two million pounds, so two million pounds will come and your mother will be wonderfully happy. Eat your breakfast.

Harry She's happy now.

George Not as happy as she will be when she's got a gold tiara, a poodle dog with diamonds in its collar, a butler, and doesn't have to be a parking-meter attendant any more. I'm surprised you aren't more pleased. Tea?

Harry I've got some.

George Then drink it.

Harry I made it and I don't feel like drinking it.

George That's a waste.

Harry Yes!

Mary, George's wife, enters. She is dressed ready for work as a parking-meter attendant

Mary (*to the audience*) I'm Mary, wife and mother, (*to George*) and has the money come yet?

Harry What d'you think?

Mary No.

Harry Right.

George Eat your boiled egg.

Harry I don't want to.

George That's what makes you bad tempered, Harry, not eating.

Harry Who do we know who's got two million pounds to spare for us?

Mary sits and eats her boiled egg

Mary There's lots of people out there who might just say, "Oh, what about sending a cheque to George and Mary Jackson, two million pounds, heard you wanted it so here it is, with love."

George Exactly.

Mary They never do though, George.

George They will.

Harry Just talk about something else.

George Just eat your egg.

Harry I'm twenty-one and I boiled it so I can do what I want with it.

Aunty Sharon enters. She is elderly but has something like a blonde beehive hairdo and is wearing a dressing-gown

Aunty Has the money come?

Mary (*to the audience*) Aunty Sharon.

Aunty And still lively, but if the money hasn't come I'll go back to bed.

The front doorbell rings

George The postman! It's the postman, and when he rings the bell it means he has a parcel! And it will contain — —

George }
Mary } (*together*) — two million pounds!

Harry It'll be blooming heavy if it does.

George Oh, my heart. It's beating like a gong!

Aunty If you're not going I will.

George No! You'll take forever. Wait, postman!

George dashes off

Aunty It's not far to the front door.

Harry He'll be disappointed again.

Mary He's never disappointed. He keeps on believing ridiculous things, an example to us all.

George rushes in carrying a parcel

George Look at this! I was right! (*He begins to tear the parcel open*)

Aunty Careful, George.

George In here — in here — are — —

Harry It isn't big enough.

Mary I don't honestly think we should count on shopping at Harrods today.

George Oh ye of little faith! It'll be — it'll be — — (*He reveals a whoopee cushion. He shakes and pushes it*)

Aunty It's a cushion.
George I'll rip it apart and see what's inside it.
Harry Let me feel it first.
George No, it's mine.
Aunty It's addressed to the family.
George And I'm the head of the family.
Harry And I am the family, so — —

Harry seizes the cushion and feels it

George Oh — —
Mary Perhaps there's a pearl necklace inside. Then I could go to the ball like
  Cinderella …
Aunty What ball?
Mary Any old ball.
Harry There's a sort of lump in it.
George Let me feel, let me feel.

Aunty Sharon takes the cushion

Aunty (*reading the cushion*) "Gentle Joyous Relaxing Cushion. Just sit on
  it anywhere, and the music will settle your shattered nerves".
George Sit on it? Not rip it open?
Mary Give it a go, Aunty Sharon.
Harry It looks like a whoopee cushion.
George Who'd be so disrespectful as to send me one of those?
Aunty My friend Terry. (*She sits on the cushion*)

The cushion farts some of Vivaldi's "Four Seasons"

Mary Oh! It's the music they play on the phone to stop you from getting
  angry.
George It doesn't work.

Aunty Sharon takes the cushion from under her

  Perhaps it's a disguise.
Aunty It's not a disguise. There's a card here and it is from Terry. (*Reading
  a card*) "To you all. Weather in Skegness is lovely. See you tomorrow."
Mary That'll be today.
Aunty (*to the audience*) Terry's my boyfriend. Him and me are what you call
  an item.
Mary They go to garden centres and remember the sixties. I suppose you
  ought to get a girlfriend, Harry.

George What's he doing, raising my hopes of great riches by sending me a silly cushion?
Aunty He's being kind.
George It's not kind. It's disappointing.
Harry Perhaps you should go to work, Dad.
George I was hoping never to go to work again. Yes, all right, it was kind. It was very kind, tell him. It really was very kind.
Mary I'll get your sandwiches and a bit of cake, love.

Mary exits

Aunty (*moving towards the exit*) If you want something hard enough, George, it'll come to you. Like I'd love a slice of toast and marmalade on a tray, if someone's going past my bedroom. And that boiled egg wouldn't go amiss if no-one wants it.
Harry (*to the audience*) I made breakfast and no-one's said thank you.
Aunty While I think of it, Harry, thank you for making breakfast — —
Harry Oh!
Aunty (*as she exits*) — and thank you for bringing it up to my room.

Aunty Sharon exits

Harry Oh. (*A slight pause; to George*) Don't be so sad, Dad.
George Sad dad. That rhymes. No, no, I'll be all right.

Harry exits

(*To the audience*) I am a little bit sad, as a matter of fact. It'll pass.

George exits

SCENE 3

Harry Jackson's office. Morning

Harry and Tracey enter. Tracey is the same age as Harry. They bring on two computers. Tracey works at her computer

Harry (*to the audience*) This is Tracey, and we work together.
Tracey (*working; to Harry*) Where've you been then?
Harry It's Dad.
Tracey Helping him collect the two million pounds, were you?
Harry It's not come.

Tracey Too heavy for the postman, was it?
Harry I've made that joke.
Tracey Couldn't get it through the letter box?
Harry All right.
Tracey Cheque bounced, cash machine jammed — —
Harry Tracey!
Tracey Oooh! Sensitive!
Harry I'm upset for him. Each day when he looks disappointed I feel I want to pick him up and cuddle him.
Tracey You're a kind boy, Harry, dreadfully boring but you are kind.
Harry Thank you.
Tracey But you have to think what you want for yourself.
Harry Will you come to the pictures with me tonight?
Tracey No.
Harry Right.
Tracey (*refering to her computer*) Oh, one of those emails that just comes out of nowhere. Junk, junk, junk.
Harry I wonder if I just sent out a message into the ether — wanted, two million pounds.
Tracey It's catching, isn't it? First your dad and now you. Try this then, just arrived in the junk. "Any help you need can be found at unicornhelp@ elysianfields.com". Sounds like you; not quite grounded.
Harry Let's see.

Mr Potter enters and crosses the stage

Mr Potter (*bossily as he crosses*) Back to your desk, lad, talking is not allowed at work.
Harry } (*together*) Yes, Mr Potter.
Tracy }
Mr Potter Talking stops you working efficiently.
Harry } (*together*) Yes, Mr Potter.
Tracy }
Mr Potter And keep smiling until tea-break when you can relax.

Mr Potter exits

Harry moves to his computer

Harry unicornhelp@elysianfields.com. There.
Tracey You're off your trolley
Harry (*typing*) Help me make my dad happy. (*To Tracey*) Where is Elysian Fields?

Tracey Somewhere up past the moon, full of shepherds in pink smocks. I've got work to do.
Harry Well, I've tried.

Harry and Tracey exit

As they exit there is a faint buzzing noise

SCENE 4

A garden centre. Lunchtime

The buzzing noise fades

Aunty Sharon enters. She is dressed in a coat and carries a lunch-box and a plastic container with a strip of petunias in it

Aunty (*to the audience*) I want you to meet my boyfriend Terry, here at the garden centre where we often have a snack amid the petunias, which I've bought some of. Terry!
Terry (*off*) Coming!
Aunty He's all there is, is Terry, but I'm very hopeful of him. Here he is.

Terry enters, wearing dated spivvy clothes

Terry My love, my flower.
Aunty My prince, my swan. How was Skegness?
Terry Empty without you. (*He kisses Aunty Sharon's hand*)
Aunty Is that all you can manage?
Terry It's my back. Did my present arrive?
Aunty What's your back?
Terry I can't bend. Did it come?
Aunty Yes, it did, and very kind, though George was disappointed. Have you strained it?
Terry I know a man who sells those cushions cheap. Yes, I strained it in the bath.
Aunty Aah.

There is a buzzing sound

Is that a hornet?

Terry Can't see, stiff neck. Shall we test that garden seat?

The buzzing sound fades

Only this morning my legs are a bit stiff. What are those?
Aunty Petunias.
Terry No, in the lunch-box.
Aunty Egg mayo.
Terry Only I've got this stomach pain — —
Aunty Oh for goodness' sake! Sometimes it's like having a used car as a boyfriend, not a human being.
Terry It's just that I'm hungry.

Terry and Aunty Sharon move to the garden seat/bench and sit

Oh, that's better.
Aunty There you are then.
Terry Very nice, and I'll have two.
Aunty You'll have to help me with the cooking when we get married.
Terry Are we getting married?
Aunty Yes. For one thing, it'd be a good example to Harry, who should be doing something about girls.
Terry There were some of those in Skegness.
Aunty And once we're married I can move out.
Terry I'll have to ask you first.
Aunty Well?
Terry It's nice just sitting here, eating.
Aunty It's not enough.
Terry We're eating sandwiches. I can't ask you to marry me when we're busy.

There is a buzzing noise like a distantly passing aeroplane

Aunty There it is again.
Terry It's my stomach calling out for another egg mayo.
Aunty It's in the sky.
Terry No, it's in my stomach, Sharon, empty and crying out for food.
Aunty It's going around the city.

The sound fades

Terry And you can buy me a cup of tea in the cafeteria — —
Aunty What?

Terry Please?
Aunty Only if we can talk about the future.
Terry I don't like the future. It's a mystery.
Aunty Then you can help me plant the petunias. (*She pulls Terry up*)
Terry With my back?
Aunty Well, I'm not waiting forever. I'm your fiancée.
Terry I've got a lot of life to live yet.

Terry and Aunty Sharon move towards the exit

Aunty. What did you get up to in Skegness?
Terry I sat in deck chairs and dreamed of your lovely way with sandwiches.
You really hurt my shoulder.

They exit

SCENE 5

A private place at George's bank. Lunchtime

*George enters. He takes a packet of sandwiches from his pocket and sits on
the bench*

George (*to the audience*) This is me, eating my lunch alone in a private place
in the bank where I work. I don't go with the other people very much
because here I can dream about what's going to happen when we have a
swimming pool and all those kitchen gadgets and a lot of sherry and a
bowling alley of our own and — and — and — —

Mr Scott enters

Mr Scott George?
George Yes, sir, Mr Scott, sir?
Mr Scott Are you all right?
George Yes, sir, Mr Scott.
Mr Scott Only as a bank manager, I like all my workers to be where I can
get in touch with them, not sitting in secret corners.
George You can always get in touch with me, sir, Mr Scott.
Mr Scott Then why d'you sit by yourself?
George My stomach rumbles. Always has, ever since I was a little boy, and
it puts other people off their food.

There is the buzzing sound like a distantly passing aeroplane

Mr Scott Is that it?
George It must be.
Mr Scott Sounds more like a buzz than a rumble.
George Some people have stomach rumble, I have stomach buzz.

The buzzing sound fades

Mr Scott The thing is I'd like you to meet me tomorrow morning in my office
to talk about your future.
George (*smiling*) Ah. My future. Yes, I'd be happy to join you tomorrow, Mr
Scott, to talk about that.
Mr Scott All right, then, George. Are you sure that was your stomach?
George Oh, yes.
Mr Scott Very unusual.

Mr Scott exits

George (*to the audience*) And tomorrow — tomorrow there'll be two
million pounds in the post so I won't need any future here at all!

The buzzing sound grows louder

I wonder what that is?

George exits

The buzzing sound dives and then is silent

SCENE 6

The Jacksons' house, Peckham. Breakfast

*Harry enters with the table laid for breakfast, including napkins; a teapot;
four boiled eggs, two of which are a darker colour than usual, and some
spoons. He sits at the table*

Harry (*to the audience*) Here we are, tomorrow has arrived, and it's
breakfast again, cooked by me again, and things might turn out a bit
differently from usual.

George enters and sits at the table

George (*to the audience*) Ah. Morning time in Peckham. And this morning,
this morning there will be two million — —

Harry (*chuckling*) Ha ha ha ha ha.
George Eat your egg.
Harry I'm too excited.
George Excited? You?

Mary enters and sits at the table

Mary Has the money come yet?
George Not yet, but Harry's excited.
Mary Eat your egg, Harry, or you'll have a mood.
Harry In a minute.

Aunty Sharon enters and sits at the table

Aunty Has the money come yet?
George Not yet.
Aunty Well, if no-one's eating that egg I could do with it.
Mary For Terry's lunch, I know.
Harry It's not going for Terry's lunch. It's mine.

Harry hits one of the darker coloured eggs with a spoon and the egg makes a loud metallic boing sound

Aha.
Sharon Terry wouldn't like an egg that made a noise.
Mary He likes a cushion that makes a noise.
George Who cooked it?
Harry I did. There were two lying on the sink side and that was from the fridge, as usual.
Mary They're a funny colour.
George Give it another go.

Harry hits the egg once more and it makes another boing sound

Sharon It's off. Throw it away.
George No. There's something in it. Hahahaha! Let me, let me. (*He grabs the egg*)

The egg makes a metallic boing sound

That's not off. It's a message, or even — perhaps it's the money! They haven't sent it through the post, they've laid it!
Harry I sent a message to a strange website yesterday and oh, Dad, it might be something in reply.

George It is! (*To the egg*) Hallo? Is there two million pounds in there?
Harry I don't think inside an egg — —
Aunty Give it another crack.
Mary It might explode
Harry It might.
George Money all over the floor. What ecstasy. (*He hits the egg hard with a spoon*)

The egg makes a hissing sound

Harry It sounds like a bomb.
George It doesn't.
Mary It does, George, move away.
Harry It could be just a chicken, very cross since I boiled it.

The egg continues to hiss

George Have confidence in yourself and your computer!

The egg explodes into two pieces. It contains a tiny figurine of Stanley

There, I told you, it's come from somewhere we know not of, and hallo, hallo? Hallo?
Mary Is the money there, George?
Harry No, it isn't.
George (*examining*) There doesn't actually seem to be anything you could exactly, as it were, describe as money in a money kind of way, but there is something that might mean something somehow. (*He picks up the figurine*)
Aunty It's one of those eggs that has things in as a surprise present.
Mary Terry probably sent it.
George No, it's a sign.
Mary Well we can't all go to Spain every other week because we've had a sign that's a little plastic man with an apron on, George, we can't.
Harry I don't think Terry could organize this. It's my computer that's done it, or Tracey's actually.
Mary Who's Tracey?
Harry A girl at work.
Aunty Are you an item?
Harry No.
Aunty Why not?

George pockets the little Stanley figurine

George There should be a message to say who it's from. What's in yours?

Mary I've not hit it yet.

George Well, do hit it.

Mary No. It might have a horror inside, like a knife that springs out at you, or a big spider, or poison gas, or — or — —

Aunty I'll have a go.

Mary Leave it!

George Come on, Mother.

Mary No! Nothing good can come of eggs that go boing and explode and have strange men in them with aprons where there should be nice soft yellow stuff.

George You're being cowardly.

Mary Yes, and I'm right. Everything's gone funny suddenly. Try your own.

George Mine looks normal.

Harry Yours could be normal, too, Mum.

Mary It's a funny colour.

George It might be part of some grand plan.

Mary That's what I'm saying. It's all right you wanting two million pounds that never comes, but Things Really Happening, Grand Plans — I don't feel comfy, George.

George It'll be all right, Mother. Hit it.

Aunty Go on, Mary. It's exciting.

Mary I don't like exciting.

George Give us a spoon. Now.

Mary hands over a spoon and George hits the egg. The egg makes a boing sound which repeats continuously

Good Lord.

Mary Stop it! Turn it off! Put a napkin over it!

Someone covers the egg with a napkin. The boing sound quietens a little

George Here's an adventure happening under our noses and you're scared?

Mary Yes.

George Well, I'm not. (*He hits the egg*) Who's in there?

The egg makes clonking and slurping noises

Mary It's a dragon, it's a dragon, I knew it was a dragon — put it in a dustbin, turn it into egg mayo for Terry, coronation chicken, anything — —

Aunty Terry won't eat that.

The egg makes a loud hissing noise

Mary (*putting her hands over her ears*) "Our Father, who art in Heaven — —"
Harry Mother!
Aunty That's new for you, isn't it?
George Shush all of you … Something remarkable is going to happen, I'm
  sure of it.

The egg pops and Harry looks under the napkin

Harry It's blown its top off. (*He removes the napkin and reveals the egg*)
Mary I won't half tell them off at Tesco's. It's organic for me from now on.
  Don't fiddle with it!

*George looks inside the egg. He pulls out a tiny figurine of the Unicorn and
a piece of paper*

George It's only another toy. A little horse.
Harry It's not a horse. It's a unicorn. There's the horn.
Mary Aaah. Sweet. I hope it's not a trap, though, George.

George pockets the Unicorn figurine

George It all means I really am going to get two million pounds and you're
  all going to look very silly. If you did this, Harry, I'm very grateful to you.
  Now, let us all go to work, perhaps for the last time and see what happens
  tonight.
Harry I certainly want to tell Tracey about this.

Harry exits

During the following, George quietly examines the piece of paper

Aunty He's kept her a secret, hasn't he?
Mary I'll go and make your sandwiches, George, and I suppose you'd like
  a few for Terry.
Aunty I'll do them. I don't want you moaning about the extra work.
Mary I never moan, Aunty Sharon, I love having you here.
Aunty You've never said.

Aunty Sharon and Mary exit

George (*reading*) "Reduced size for internet travel. Add water and we'll
  begin to grow back instantly. Looking forward to meeting you. Stanley."
  Stanley? Well — — (*He pours some tea from the teapot into his pocket*

containing the figurines. He then delves his hand into this pocket and produces a larger Stanley as a glove puppet on to the edge of the table)
Good heavens.
Stanley's Voice Good-morning...
George Good-morning.
Stanley's Voice Are you well?
George Actually, I'm meeting Mr Scott this morning to talk about the future — —
Stanley's Voice I'd better stay out of sight until that's settled, then.

George disappears the puppet Stanley back into his pocket

Oh. Right. (*To the audience*) How extraordinary. How utterly amazing. Here we go then, Mr Scott, and perhaps we'll see what the future really has in store.

George exits

SCENE 7

Harry Jackson's office. Morning

Tracy sits at her computer

Harry enters

Tracey Oh, you're on time.
Harry Yes.
Tracey The two million arrived has it?
Harry No. A unicorn in a boiled egg.
Tracey Your brains boiled with it, were they?
Harry Something did arrive, Tracey, and it came from that website of yours. Who knows what the future has in store for us now? Will you come to the pictures with me?
Tracey It all sounds a bit peculiar to me.
Harry At least will you come home after work and see what we got in the hard-boiled eggs?
Tracey You joking?
Harry There could be a lot of money in this, Trace. Swimming pools, trips to Spain, little dogs with diamond collars, sherry — —
Tracey You really mean this?
Harry I don't know what I mean. Breakfast was almost mystic.
Mr Potter (*off*) No talking!

Tracy
Harry } (*together*) No, Mr Potter.

Mr Potter (*off*) Keep smiling.

Tracy
Harry } (*together*) Yes, Mr Potter.

Tracey What happened exactly?

Harry Come home after work and see.

Tracey It wouldn't mean anything serious, like going to the pictures?

Harry No.

Mr Potter (*off*) Are you smiling, workers?

Harry Yes, Mr Potter.

Harry and Tracey exit

Scene 8

George's bank. Morning

George enters, wrestling with the Unicorn

The Unicorn is a hand-puppet which is operated like the famous Emu puppet — the mouth being operated by George's hand and the body covering his arm. It burrows under George's jacket, delves into his inside pocket and then emerges with a sandwich. It disappears back up inside the jacket to eat the sandwich hidden somewhere around George's armpit

George This bit should be me meeting with Mr Scott to talk about my future, but everybody's been growing a bit fast and it might be difficult. What are you up to? Come out. Come out!

Mr Scott enters

Mr Scott Ah, George. Would you like to pop into my office?

George I'm sorry, Mr Scott, but circumstances have arisen which — —

Mr Scott Your stomach buzzing again?

George No, we seem to have got past that and into boiled eggs — no, beyond boiled eggs — —

Mr Scott Boiled eggs?

George Breakfast. Things came that we didn't quite expect — well, I did, but the others — Ow.

Mr Scott Have you something under your jacket?

George Yes, a fortune probably.

Mr Scott Not a load of stolen bank notes, I hope, ha,ha.

George Ha,ha.

Mr Scott People say you do talk a lot about two million pounds.
George And I may be about to get them. Ooh!
Mr Scott George?
George I'll tell you the honest truth, Mr Scott. There's a unicorn been growing in my jacket and it's had my sandwiches.
Mr Scott Really?
George And there's a man with a green apron in there, too, had a go at the cake I shouldn't wonder. However, they're probably going to make me very rich indeed.
Mr Scott Perhaps we don't need this meeting, then, George. Just go home, and I'll write you a letter.
George What about?
Mr Scott Well, if you have a fortune under there you don't need a job, do you? And you do disturb things here, eating by yourself, bringing unicorns to work, talking about boiled eggs and funny stomach noises and two million pounds. I think we may both be happier if you left. I'll write you a nice letter to say you're free to be unusual somewhere else. Goodbye.

Mr Scott exits

George You mean I'm fired?

The Unicorn comes out of George's jacket and gazes at George

Well, it's what I've always wanted, provided there was cash — I mean — I hope you'll have some ideas. Perhaps we'll just go home for tea, and talk about what to do next, shall we? Mother? Mother!

The Unicorn dives for another sandwich

Aunty (*off*) She's at the shops, George.
George Well things are happening, Aunty Sharon. Ouch!

George exits

SCENE 9

The Jacksons' house, Peckham. Teatime

Aunty Sharon enters. She pushes on a table laid with Jaffa cakes, teacups, a teapot and various other things. She places the whoopee cushion on one of the chairs

Aunty (*as she enters; calling out*) I thought you were having a meeting with Mr Scott?
George (*off*) I was, but he said he wanted to write me a letter.
Aunty Who to?
George (*off*) Me I think … Get off. There are no more sandwiches.
Aunty Why would he write to you if you were there?
George (*off*) To say how pleased he is that I might get two million pounds.
Aunty Where from?
George (*off*) There's things happening.

Harry and Tracey enter

Harry Hallo, Aunty Sharon. This is Aunty Sharon.
Tracey Hallo, Aunty Sharon. This is Tracey from work.
Aunty Are you an item?
Tracey No!
Aunty I'm an item with my friend Terry.
Harry We aren't like that at all.
Tracey It's just that Harry said would I like to see what happened at breakfast.
Aunty Boiled eggs. Have a Jaffa cake while you tell us about you and Harry being an item.
Tracey Is this some sort of game?
Harry Aunty Sharon we're not an item.
George (*off*) Keep your nose to yourself for heaven's sake!
Harry Are you all right, Dad?
George (*off*) Control him! Yow!

George enters running. He is followed by the enthusiastic Unicorn and Stanley. The Unicorn is operated by two actors

Careful! That thing's sharp!

The Unicorn canters round the stage happily swinging his horn and causing the others to scream and shout

Harry What's happened?
Aunty It was a doll at breakfast time.
George Well, it's not now.
Stanley Now then, now then, just calm down and don't get over excited. Could he have one of those cake things?
George He's had my sandwiches already.
Aunty When?

George When he was in my pocket.
Tracey You never had all that in your pocket.
George They were little, and they grew. (*To Tracey*) How d'you do.

The Unicorn searches for a Jaffa cake on the table and a cup and saucer crash to the ground

Harry Mind the teapot!

The Unicorn knocks over one of the chairs. Tracey hides behind Stanley

Aunty They were both so sweet this morning.
Stanley If someone could just get the cake while I stroke him.
Harry Here. There's a good boy.
Tracey (*coming out from behind Stanley*) Are you part of this?
Stanley I'm the person who keeps the golden horns dusted — twenty-four carat — name of Stanley, worker in the Elysian Fields, up past the moon, where the email came to. I'm here to help.
George I don't mean to be inquisitive, look a gift horse in the mouth, as it were, but why did someone send a large unicorn to a small house in Peckham?
Stanley In answer to your email.
George What did your email say, Harry?
Harry Send something to make my dad happy.
George I don't want to be happy. I want to be rich. Well, rich and happy, if possible.
Aunty That horn'd be worth a couple of million if you could get it off.

The Unicorn turns on Aunty Sharon with anger

Stanley Careful, they're sensitive.
Aunty It was just a thought, sweetheart, I didn't mean it.
Stanley Is there another cake?
Tracey I'll get it. (*She moves to the table for a Jaffa cake*)
Stanley Oh.

Tracey holds out the Jaffa cake. The Unicorn stops moving and stares at her. It shakes its head very slowly, and then very gently paws the ground

Tracey What's the matter with him?
Stanley Girls, probably — I thought this might happen. There aren't any proper girls in the Elysian Fields, only shepherdesses, so he's what you might call dazzled. As the French say, *un coup de foudre*.

George What?
Aunty Love at first sight.
Harry Careful, Trace.
Aunty But she can't be an item with a unicorn. Does he bite?
Stanley No. He tosses people about.
Tracey He won't harm me. He's sweet.
Harry Yes, well, just see that spike doesn't go in your face.
George I know I'm asking a lot of questions, but now he knows that what I really want is — is …
Stanley Two million pounds, yes, we heard when you lost your job.
Harry You lost your job?
George I don't need a job if I'm rich — I am going to be rich, aren't I? I mean what's he going to do? Is he going to give us that — thing on his forehead?

The Unicorn reacts

I didn't say horn, I didn't say horn!
Stanley Mr Jackson — —
George Well I do want to know what he's going to do. I've a family to support, and dreams to fulfil.
Stanley Well, he can do bits of magic to impress people. Come on, impress.

The Unicorn produces several bouquets of flowers and gives them to Tracey and Aunty Sharon

Aunty Oh. (*Pleased*) Saucy thing!
George They won't make us wealthy. Is that all he plans to do?
Stanley It is a bit tacky really, when you think how he shrank us to fit those egg things, but perhaps it's Peckham. I mean it's not the Elysian Fields, is it, when it comes to magic making.
George Of course it's wonderful to have a unicorn of one's own — —

The Unicorn looks cross

Sorry! What did I say? What did I say?!

Stanley holds the Unicorn with some difficulty

Stanley He's not yours. He's just come to give you help.
George But how?
Stanley I don't know! Now do stop annoying him, it's wearing me out, keeping the peace.

Aunty Mary's going to have a shock when she gets back. There aren't many
parking-meter people who have a legendary animal in their living-room.
Does he have a name?

Stanley They don't do names in the Elysian Fields.

Aunty Oh, poor thing. I'll call him Alfred, because of the Jaffa cakes. No?
I'll give it a think and talk about it later.

George And then perhaps — later — we can also talk about the — er ——
the help he came to give us. Is he listening?

The Unicorn gazes at Tracey

Harry No. He's harassing Tracey.

Tracey He's lovely.

Harry (*slapping the Unicorn*) Stop it. Stop it!

*The Unicorn turns angrily knocking over another chair, the teapot and
possibly pushing the entire table over*

Tracey Harry!

Stanley (*to Harry*) You shouldn't have done that. (*To the Unicorn*) Stop it!
You'll frighten everyone. You'll frighten the girl.

The Unicorn stops rampaging

(*To Tracey*) What's your name, love ? If you don't mind me asking.

Tracey Tracey.

Stanley Well you're a calming influence anyway, Tracey. Unlike some
people.

Aunty How about Simon? Henry? Arbuthnot? I'll keep trying.

The Unicorn turns to gaze at Tracey again

Tracey Aaah. I think he'd like another Jaffa cake. Harry?

*Harry takes a Jaffa cake from the table or if it has been knocked over finds
a Jaffa cake on the floor*

Harry (*throwing the Jaffa cake to Tracey*) That was my tea.

Aunty (*to the Unicorn*) Who's a spoilt boy then? (*She strokes the Unicorn*)

Tracey gives the Jaffa cake to the Unicorn. The Unicorn nuzzles her

Tracey He's lovely.

Harry Huh.

George He's going to cost a fortune to keep. That's the last Jaffa.

Stanley Is that your garden out there?

Aunty I'm the one that plants the flowers.

Stanley He might settle comfily if we put him out there.

George Listen, it's just … I mean the thing is, there's the new car, and the trips to Spain, and the little dog with the diamonds in its collar, and the kitchen gadgets, sherry — —

Stanley You'll just have to wait till he makes up his mind about all that. There's no rushing unicorns, stubborn as concrete — well you are, and you know me and I know you so don't give me any of that. If I could just take him out into the garden, I'll come back when I've settled him down. And I'm very fond of a ham supper, if you've got one, with potato salad with a poached egg on top. And can I call you George?

Stanley leads the Unicorn and they exit

George The cheek. Ham supper, Jaffa cakes — where's the money coming from? Mother's wages as a meter lady?

Tracey (*calling off*) Sleep well, Unicorn.

Harry I'm sorry, Dad, I didn't expect this to happen when I sent the email.

George Computers never do what you expect.

Aunty (*to Tracey*) Are you all right, love?

Tracey Yes, fine.

Aunty You look a bit flummoxed.

Tracey I've just never seen anything like him before.

Harry Shall I take you home?

Tracey I'm all right!

Harry You do look a bit flummoxed.

Tracey There's no need to make a big deal out of this. I just saw my first unicorn, that's all. It's been nice meeting you all.

Mary (*off*) Who the bleeding heck let this thing into my garden! Get off. Go away. And those are Aunty Sharon's flowers.

Harry Mother! Language!

Stanley (*off*) Don't upset him!

Aunty Don't let him eat my petunias.

Mary enters

Mary I warned you at breakfast, George Jackson. It isn't normal and I said so, and we've had a visitation of a monster because you interfered with the way things ought to be. And who are you? Another complication?

Harry She's Tracey from work.

Tracey I'm Tracey from work.

Mary Well, if you and Harry are what Aunty Sharon calls an item you've started at the wrong moment. George get rid of that unicorn and get me a Jaffa cake. I can't cope.

Aunty There are none.

Mary Where are they?

George Down the unicorn.

Mary It's your unicorn so you can go and buy some more Jaffa cakes.

George It's not my unicorn it's Harry's.

Harry I wanted to help.

Mary And look at my china. I don't want all this, George. I don't want a little dog and visits to Spain.

Aunty He's lost his job as well.

Mary (*on the verge of tears*) Oh! You really are so careless!

George It'll turn out all right, Mother.

Terry enters

Terry Have you seen what's in your garden, missis?

Mary I have, and it's done all this to my crockery and eaten all my food. I'm living in a world of disaster.

Terry There's two million quid's worth of unicorn horn out there.

George There is. There is.

Aunty You're not to say things like that, Terry. It's a beautiful creature, not to be vandalized, and I'm going to choose a name for it.

Mary It's a monster. (*Looking up to the heavens*) And I'm sorry for all the wicked things I've done, if I have done wicked things, so please just take the unicorn away!

Terry I'm only telling the truth. Get that golden horn off his head and you and George could buy the Queen Elizabeth.

George We could, and sail round the world forever.

Tracey No.

Terry Who are you?

Tracey I'm a friend of Harry's.

Aunty They're an item.

Harry No, we're not!

Mary Good.

Tracey That lovely creature doesn't want to lose its golden horn, so don't suggest it.

Mary Oh! Attitude!

Terry I know a man would take some unicorn horn and not ask any questions.

Aunty You always know someone who won't ask questions, and if you try to take that horn, you'll end up on the end of it. I'm going to get a cup of camomile.

Aunty exits

Mary I'm terrified to go into my own garden, so, you got it in here, Harry, you get it out. Find me an aspirin, Aunty Sharon! And you, leave my boy alone. He's too young to be itemized.

Mary exits

Harry Mum!
Tracey I think I would like you to take me home, Harry. I do feel a bit funny.
Harry All right.
Tracey It doesn't mean anything.
Harry (*resigned*) No.

Harry and Tracey exit

Terry Can I stay for tea?
George There isn't any.
Terry You've got a fortune on your lawn. You'll be able to buy a load of take-aways tomorrow.
George The trouble is ... The trouble is — it's not as simple as what I meant.
Terry Things never are.
George But it's got to work somehow. You can't just have a fortune sleeping in your garden and let it go. It's mine, it must be mine! But while it's on its forehead, it isn't mine, so what are we going to do? (*He sits down on the chair with the whoopee cushion*)

The cushion farts some of Vivaldi's "Four Seasons" and George leaps up

Oh this silly cushion. Couldn't you have found a decent one?
Terry I know a man'll get me another.
George (*distracted*) I have to have that horn. I have to! I've got no job!

Black-out

ACT II

SCENE 1

The Jacksons' garden. Early evening

The Lights come up on a row of petunias and some chairs placed to form a garden bench. On the bench is the whoopee cushion

Aunty Sharon enters with a trowel and a very small watering-can

Aunty (*to the audience*) It's early evening now and this is the garden. I've come to look at my petunias and do a bit of weeding. (*She kneels down by the petunias and, weeds and waters them*) Really, I'd like to get another glimpse of that young unicorn, because I've thought of a name for him. And also I'd like to get a glimpse of that Stanley, in a cautious sort of way, because you have to admit, he's better built than Terry.

Stanley enters

Talk of the devil.
Stanley Good-evening.
Aunty Yes.
Stanley It's Stanley.
Aunty Yes.
Stanley Why don't you say. "Hallo, Stanley, what a very nice name for a very nice person?"
Aunty Don't push your luck. I'm taken at the moment.
Stanley I was only being friendly.
Aunty They all say that. It is a nice name.

Stanley sits

Stanley It's a nice little garden. Not quite the Elysian Fields, of course, a bit short of crystal fountains and humming birds, but cosy.
Aunty Aren't you tired after that journey?
Stanley People guarding precious animals sleep very little. It's a hard life.
Aunty Oh dear. Could you do with help, then?
Stanley It does get lonely with only unicorns to talk to. They don't say much, just the odd whisper when they feel urgent.
Aunty I could talk to you if I took a job up there, in the Thingummy Fields.
Stanley I rather like it down here, really. Ham suppers and that. Cosy gardens.

Aunty Oh, yes? We'd better think then, hadn't we?

Stanley What about?

Aunty Well — —

George enters holding a saw behind his back

George Ah! Good-evening. Is your four footed friend — er ... Is he asleep, is he?

Stanley In the potting shed.

George Among the garden shears and pruning knifes, ha,ha? Deep in slumber and happy dreams?

Aunty (*still weeding*) What are you doing with that saw, George?

George Saw? Oh, good heavens. I wonder what it's doing, hiding there behind my back.

Stanley Don't you know?

George Well, I expect it was going to cut down a few trees, shorten a few planks, cut up some vegetables, that sort of thing to pass a pleasant evening.

Aunty To cut off a unicorn's horn, maybe.

Stanley Ooh no.

George Well, I hadn't thought of that, Aunty Sharon. What an idea, a considerable idea, now you mention it.

Stanley I couldn't let you do it, though.

George Couldn't you? The thing is, he's here to make me rich, isn't he?

Stanley To make you happy.

George Yes, happy, happy, I keep forgetting. But it doesn't make me happy to have that great golden conk in my garden which I could sell for about two million pounds, from which I can't raise a brass farthing while it's attached to that animal's forehead.

Stanley It stays there.

George Well, I could go in and ask him about that, couldn't I. "Hallo, Unicorn," I could say, "Can I saw your horn off?" And he could say — —

Stanley Buzz off.

George Why?

Stanley Because it's his, and it might hurt a bit.

George So the best thing would be just to have a quick saw while he's snoring away, anaesthetized as it were — snore, snore, snore, saw, saw, saw and Bob's your uncle, trips to Spain and a new car.

Aunty He'd wake up and skewer you.

George Then why's he here, driving me mad with greed!? Well, not greed, I just want a reasonable living, and he could — I want it off, and sold and a load of lolly in the bank!

Silence

Well?

Aunty That sounded very nasty.

George I'm not nasty, I'm normal.

Aunty Even as a little boy — —

George I was a lovely little boy!

Aunty You should just feel honoured that you have him as a visitor.

George Yes. Yes, yes of course. And I'm not nasty.

Stanley So leave him alone like your Aunty Sharon says.

George She's not my Aunty Sharon, she's Mother's and she never knew me as a little boy.

Aunty I did!

George You didn't!

Aunty And I'm thinking of taking a job looking after the unicorns in the Whatsername Fields.

George You can't do that. Once you're there, you'd never get back, would she?

Stanley Probably not.

George No.

Aunty Well, Terry's not coming forward with a wedding-ring, and the unicorn's ever so pleasant, and the staff are personable.

Stanley Me?

Aunty So — —

George Pleasant isn't enough! I forbid you to leave Peckham and our happy family. We'd miss you. Who'd do the washing up?

Aunty Then put down that saw and I might reconsider.

George Oh. Right. I — I ... I'll just go and hang it up in the shed. No, I promise. I won't — I won't do anything surgical. I do promise.

George exits humming quietly to himself

Aunty (*getting up*) Go and see what he's up to.

Stanley Nothing, he promised.

Aunty He's seen the gold.

Stanley No-one's ever called me personable before. Does that mean I am nice?

Aunty How's your back?

Stanley My back?

Aunty A girl can't wait forever, and Terry's just a mass of torn ligaments.

A smash is heard off stage

George enters backwards. He is pursued by a very cool-looking Unicorn with the saw hooked by its handle over his horn. The Unicorn pushes George on to Aunty's petunias

George You completely misunderstood. I was just going to hang the saw up and I tripped over you. It's lovely having you here as a visitor. Couldn't be nicer. We're honoured.
Stanley You've brought on his coolness mode.
Aunty Mind your feet on my flowers, George.

The Unicorn forces him off the flowers

And the watering-can ...
George Stanley, he's going to do something dreadful.
Stanley It looks as if you were going to do something dreadful.
Aunty You wouldn't do something dreadful to our George, would you?

The Unicorn looks as if he would do something dreadful

Oh, you have got his dander up.
Stanley I think you should apologize, Mr Jackson.
George What for?
Stanley Using that.

The Unicorn throws down the saw

George He took it before I had a chance to do — all right, all right, I apologize! But — just listen — I would like you to know what you're going to do to make us ri ... Happy.

The Unicorn thinks

What is he up to?
Stanley He's thinking, which at this moment could be dangerous.
George More dangerous?
Stanley Much more.

The Unicorn suddenly laughs silently

Yes. That means he's got an idea in his head that he's going to be clever about. Come on, love, whisper it to me, your old friend Stanley, who's known you ever since you were a foal.

The Unicorn shakes his head

Oh come on, whisper.
George Go on, whisper — whisper, whisper, whisper to Stanley Wanley how you're going to make Georgie Porgie happy.

The Unicorn shakes his head vehemently several times

Stanley What else did you do out there?

George I only suggested that he should shed his horns like stags do, or deer, or whatever it is — No, no, I'm sorry, it was a foolish thought, very silly.

Aunty You're a fool, George.

George I'm practical, and always was, even as a little boy.

Aunty Now then, Arthur — I'm going to call you Arthur, Arthur Unicorn, everyone has to have a name — What are you going to do to make George happy?

Stanley Oh Arthur, like the king with all those knights round the table. Tell Stanley, then, Arthur.

The Unicorn whispers into Stanley's ear

He says you'll find out soon, and he likes the flowers.

Aunty Aah. (*She kisses the Unicorn*)

George Find out soon? How long is soon?

The Unicorn gives George a gentle push with his horn on to the bench with the whoopee cushion

Sorry, sorry. (*He sits on the whoopee cushion*)

The cushion farts the tune of Vivaldi's "Four Seasons"

Ow.

Stanley Careful. You could easily slip. It has happened before, guts everywhere. Now come along to bed and I'll read you a story before you go to sleep.

Stanley and the Unicorn exit. As they leave, the Unicorn puts its tongue out at George

Aunty Aren't they sweet?

George He could've done me a very nasty injury. D'you think he's planning to do something — peculiar?

Aunty It's all peculiar. I like that.

George It could be really awful, like turning us all into snakes and toads.

Aunty Get off, go to bed and don't be fanciful. There's tomorrow's breakfast to be ready for, and perhaps it'll be like everyone else's, quiet, reading the papers.

George You'd better take the flowers in.

George exits

Aunty I'll have to make up my mind about Terry. He's very kind by nature, if slow. But I do like that Stanley, though he needs mothering a bit. I'm taking in the flowers because the next part will be tomorrow morning, probably, and indoors.

SCENE 2

The Jacksons' house. Breakfast

Stanley enters. He pushes on the table laid with breakfast including a bread knife, toast and marmalade. He places the whoopee cushion on one of the chairs

Stanley (*to the audience*) Morning time. I had to get my own breakfast, no-one's about.

George enters wearing a tea-towel over his head. He is trying to hide his face from Stanley

Oh.Good-morning.
George Morning. Did you sleep well?
Stanley Yes. In the shed. Do you have any cornflakes and syrup?
George For you?
Stanley For Arthur. I don't suppose you have any Ambrosia?
George Ambrosia — no, I don't — —
Stanley D'you know you've got a tea-towel over your head?
George Yes, I do.
Stanley Is that how you eat breakfast down here?
George Not usually, no. (*He moves towards the exit*) Cornflakes and syrup.
Stanley And is there tea?
George I expect so. I don't know where Harry is. (*Calling off*) Mother?
Mary (*off*) Coming.

Mary enters wearing a tea-towel over her head

Is that George?
George Yes. Is that you?
Mary Something surprising happened to me in the night, George.
George It did to me, as well.
Mary Let's see.

George unveils to reveal a unicorn horn on his forehead

(*Shrieking*) It's the same as me! (*She unveils to reveal a unicorn horn on her forehead*) George!

George Mary!

Mary It's worse than anything I expected!

George Oh heavens!

They rush to hug for comfort but their horns get in the way

George Stop. We'll do ourselves a mischief.

Mary You see? This is where your fantasy has got us.

George I didn't do it.

Stanley Oh dear, oh dear, oh dear. Arthur's been really silly.

Mary He's been wicked, and monstrous and utterly thoughtless. How are we going to face the neighbours?

Stanley I have to say it rather suits you.

Mary Suits me? Where's a mirror? Harry?

Harry (*off*) I'll bring one.

George Mother, I don't think it is entirely my fault.

Mary It is, (*to Stanley*) and yours and that creature's, everybody's fault but mine. I can't reach my husband.

Stanley You actually look rather chic.

Mary Chic my eye! These things are like something out of a cracker.

George (*amused*) Or an ice-cream cone.

Stanley If the worst comes to the worst — —

Mary Which it will — —

Stanley — you could always use them for that, put your scoop in your own cornet.

Stanley laughs. Mary doesn't

No, but it's serious. You aren't going to be popular on the tube.

Mary We're going to be miserable for the rest of our lives, our whole wretched lives.

George No, Mother, there's always a solution.

Stanley Is there cornflakes and syrup?

Mary Is that a solution?

Stanley Arthur's always cross till he's had his breakfast, so if I feed him — —

Mary (*calling off*) Harry, cornflakes and syrup for our tormentor.

Harry (*off*) Wait a second.

Mary We've all the time in the world. I can't stick tickets on windscreens looking like this.

Harry enters carrying a bowl of cornflakes and a mirror. He, too, has a unicorn horn on his forehead

Harry Here's the mirror and the food, and Stanley, you've got to speak to that animal. We've been facially challenged. How can I ever get close enough to Tracey now to give her a kiss?
Mary You can't, your father and I have tried. And anyway, I took against her.
Harry Why?
Mary Everything became too much for me.
Stanley I'd better speak to him at once but I can't promise anything certain.

Stanley takes the bowl and Mary takes the mirror from Harry

Harry exits

George Just ask him what the point is. (*He laughs*)
Mary (*holding up the mirror*) D'you know, if it wasn't for the weight I'd quite fancy myself with this.
Harry It makes you unapproachable.
Mary Yes. People do stick pins in themselves, don't they, and this is more genteel.
Harry Mother, be your age.
George Perhaps we can get them taken off at the doctor's.
Mary It makes me feel quite mythical.
Harry Mother.

Aunty Sharon screams off stage

Aunty (*off*) I've turned into an elephant! Someone's stuck a trumpet on my forehead! I've been tampered with appallingly!

Aunty Sharon enters. She has the biggest of the unicorn horns on her forehead

Get this off! (*She swings the horn about narrowly missing hitting the others*)
Mary Be careful, Aunty Sharon.
Aunty I don't want to be careful, I want to be free. I don't mind going to the Whatsit Fields as a guard, but not as a unicorn. Do something, George.
George (*dodging Aunty Sharon's unicorn horn*) Oooops. That is worth a penny or two.
Mary We just have to learn how to be graceful, Aunty Sharon.

Aunty It's too late for me to do that. Operate, George. Here's the bread knife. (*She takes the bread knife from the table and gives it to George*)

George Perhaps that's the plan, to harvest our own horns. You first, and then — and then — I can take it to the bank.

Aunty It's my horn, so it'll be my bank.

George It's my skill, so it will be my bank.

Aunty My bank.

George My bank. Unless you'd like to operate on yourself? (*He offers Aunty Sharon the knife*)

Aunty Don't mess me about.

Mary I'd keep it if I were you. We do look rather smart.

Aunty You look a fool. So, acts of mercy first, George. Greed second. Get this horn off my head.

George And then I'll take it to the bank? My bank?

Aunty And after that I'll operate on you, and it'll be my bank.

George That's possible.

Harry We can each keep our own, Dad.

George Quite likely. Ready?

Harry Dad? I got this unicorn.

Aunty Tracey gave you the address.

George And no-one would've got anywhere if it hadn't been for me and my plans, new car, meaty barbecues, sherry. I'll operate first and then we can talk about who has the money later.

Harry We'll all share it.

George Yes, of course. Get a sticking-plaster someone.

Mary Scalpel, nurse.

Mary exits and shortly returns with a sticking-plaster

George Sit down, Aunty Sharon.

Aunty Sharon sits down on the whoopee cushion. The whoopee cushion farts some of Vivaldi's "Four Seasons" and she jumps up bumping her horn into George's eye

Harry I'll operate. (*He moves the cushion*)

George No, it's all right, I'll manage with one eye.

Aunty Will you be able to see?

George Certainly. Here we go. Hold her still you two.

Mary I'd be lovely on television.

They all have difficulty avoiding each others' horns as they gather around Aunty Sharon

George This won't hurt, Aunty. Steady, I don't want to chop her head off. (*He begins to saw at the horn*)

Aunty Careful, it is hurting.

George No, it's not.

Aunty Yes, it is.

George It's not.

Aunty How d'you know?

George Because I do.

Harry She could be right, Dad.

George She rarely is.

Harry She might be this time.

George It is not hurting!

Harry It's her forehead.

George And very thick.

Mary I'm keeping mine the way it is.

George Who's ever seen a public servant with a horn on her brow? There'll be traffic accidents, cyclists will bump into you, photos in the *News of the World* — —

Stanley enters

Stanley He says you've got to decide for yourselves how to deal ... What are you doing?

George It's called creating liquidity. Or getting rich ... Happy.

Stanley Not like that. This is my favourite Aunty Sharon, who's going to look after me in the Elysian Fields.

Aunty Get your horn out of my eye, George.

George Get yours out of mine, because it's the only one working.

Stanley Stop it! Stop! (*He looks as if he might cry*)

Aunty Sharon's horn comes off

Aunty It's all right, Stanley.

George There. Sticking-plaster, and utter, utter triumph! Two million pounds at the very least.

Aunty Mine.

George Mine.

Aunty Sharon and George have a tug of war with the horn

Aunty Harry said we keep our own.

Stanley (*grabbing the horn*) You're not to quarrel. It's lovely here, and you mustn't fight.

Terry enters

Terry What's happening to my flower?

Aunty I'm perfectly all right. I've been de-horned like an old sheep, that's all.

Terry You look like a herd of rhinos. (*To Stanely*) Were you responsible for this?

Stanley The unicorn.

Terry takes hold of the golden unicorn horn

Terry Well, I'm responsible for all this, because she's my — my — my ...

Aunty Fiancée?

They all look at Terry

Terry I didn't say that.

Stanley She's my special friend, and she shall have it. (*He grabs the horn*)

George And I was the doctor who cut it off. (*He grabs the horn*)

Terry grabs the horn

Terry I gave you the idea that you could sell it, and since I know a man who — —

George Sit on your calming cushion and have some toast and marmalade.

George pushes Terry on to the whoopee cushion and grabs the horn from him. The cushion farts some of Vivaldi's "Four Seasons"

There! Now all of you be calm while I go to the bank.

George exits

Harry Is that what Arthur expected?

Stanley I don't know.

Aunty Let's go and find a cup of camomile, and talk about the future. (*She moves towards the exit*)

Harry This is the future.

Stanley Well, that was breakfast, anyway.

Aunty And Mary will make Terry some egg mayo if he asks for it.

Harry, Stanley and Aunty Sharon exit

Mary (*drifting towards the exits*) I won't, I won't ...

Mary exits

Terry (*to the audience*) This isn't the way things were yesterday.

Terry moves towards the exit with the cushion

(*As he exits*) I know a man who might help.

Terry exits

SCENE 3

London. Morning

There is the sound of a tube train

Members of the cast play various different passengers travelling on the tube train. They wear coats and have newspapers, etc.

George enters with his horn still growing from his forehead and wearing an eyepatch. He carries Aunty Sharon's unicorn horn

During the following, George boards the tube and joins the rest of the cast with some difficulty, bashing into people with his horn and causing general mayhem. The cast mime moving on a tube as it travels along and slows down, etc.

George This is me on the tube going to the bank. Sorry. Excuse me.
Female Passenger What do you think you're doing?
George Nothing.
Male Passenger Are you going to a party, or what?
George No, it's just that — —
Female Passenger If you think that's nothing — —

George knocks the newspaper out of a male passenger's hands

Male Passenger That's my newspaper.
George (*picking up the newspaper and handing it to the passenger*) I'm so sorry. Here.
Male Passenger Ouch. That hurt.
Female Passenger You're a danger to us all.

The tube begins to slow

Male Passenger Get out and walk.
Female Passenger Go on, get out. Get out.
George I'm about to be a millionaire.
Male Passenger And I'm about to call the police.
Female Passenger Did you steal that?
George Of course not, and I've two more stops to go.

The train stops

Passengers Out. Go on out!

   Other members of the cast enter and wait to get on the tube train

New Passenger Some people ought to be kept indoors.

George steps out of the train and the other passengers board the tube

George I'm going to be a millionaire.

The train departs. George walks one way as the passengers on the train mime travelling off the other way

   I'm going to be a millionaire! I'm going to be a millionaire! I'm going to
   be a millionaire! I'm going to be a millionaire!

   George and the Passengers exit

SCENE 4

Peckham. Morning

Harry and Tracey enter carrying folders in their hands as if going to their office. She is looking at the horn on Harry's forehead

Tracey Come off it. He's too sweet to play that sort of trick on you. It must
   be a disease, like acne.
Harry It's not. He's very moody.
Tracey Well, cooped up in that garden. I'll take him for a walk after work.
Harry In Peckham?
Tracey We'll go up Telegraph Hill.
Harry I'd feel like a fool.
Tracey You can stay at home, then. With Mummy and Daddy.

Mr Potter enters or just his voice is heard

Mr Potter Nobody's allowed to work here wearing horns, Harry. Off you go and see a vet. The rest of you smile quietly at your computer screen.

Mr Potter exits

Tracey You'd better go.
Harry You're silly about this animal. You're just like Aunty Sharon, calling him Arthur.

Harry exits

Tracey That's a lovely name for him. He's lovely.

Tracey exits

SCENE 5

The bank. Morning

George enters carrying Aunty Sharon's unicorn horn and wearing the eyepatch

George (*to the audience*) This is the greatest moment of my life, new furniture, lovely garden, shopping at Harrods …

Mr Scott enters

Mr Scott I thought I fired you, George. (*He sees George's horn on his forehead*) Oh! Are you ill?
George What I want to talk to you about — —
Mr Scott Can you squeeze it, like a pimple?
George It's gold. Twenty-four carat. And so's this. (*He shows Aunty Sharon's horn*)
Mr Scott It's the two million pound thing, gone to your head. (*He laughs*)

George hands Aunty Sharon's unicorn horn over

George I want to bank it.
Mr Scott Where'd you get it?
George Off Aunty Sharon's forehead.
Mr Scott You stole it.
George She gave me permission.

Mr Scott The first thing I shall have to do is ring the police to find out what you've done with the rest of Aunty Sharon.

George She's at home, drinking camomile tea.

Mr Scott The second thing I shall have to do is have it fingerprinted in case it came from a museum.

George I've told you — —

Mr Scott The third thing, I'll have to send it to head office to find out what it's worth, and then I'll have to go to the law courts to decide who owns it, and probably it'll end up in the pockets of lawyers.

George No, give it back! It's a unicorn horn that grew on Aunty Sharon's forehead!

Mr Scott and George tussle with the horn

Mr Scott (*calling*) Ring 999, somebody! George Jackson's either having a delusion or else he's guilty of something very nasty.

George Give it to me. Give — it — to — me!

The unicorn horn falls and skewers George's foot into the ground. George tugs at the horn uselessly

Ow!

Mr Scott (*running towards the exit*) It's all right, I've got him pinned. Get the police.

Mr Scott exits

George Nothing's ever simple. I don't know why it is, but it's never simple and it should be. (*He pulls the horn out of his foot and limps towards the exit*)

Mr Scott (*off*) Come back! Stop thief!

George (*as he goes*) I'm not a thief and I'm going home. And I'm not one bit happy, and I wish I was.

George exits

SCENE 6

Telegraph Hill. Evening

Stanley, Terry and Aunty Sharon enter. Terry carries a paperbag

Aunty (*to the audience*) Evening on Telegraph Hill, and it's been one heck of a climb. How's everybody's backs?

Terry ⎱ (*together; with varying confidence*) Fine.
Stanley ⎰
Aunty (*to the audience*) Arthur's disappeared, and Harry says that Tracey must've taken him for a walk up here. He's not come himself because he says they're not an item.
Terry He wants to be an item, but he thinks perhaps — —
Aunty. Never mind what he thinks, it's quite important that we find the unicorn, because — —
Stanley They're coming.
Terry Oh good, I've got this present they might like.
Aunty If I can finish? (*To the audience*) Because you never know when a unicorn can lose its temper.
Stanley If we could just keep out of sight? He might be all right, you see, and we don't want to get his dander up again. Just over here.
Terry (*to the audience*) I have got this present from a man I know — —
Aunty Terry! You heard.
Terry (*sotto voce*) Bossy boots.

Terry, Aunty and Stanley move to one side and are, as it were, invisible to Tracey and the Unicorn

Tracey and the Unicorn enter. The Unicorn has a petunia in his mouth

Tracey There. There's lots of space for you to run around here.

The Unicorn runs around

You look as free as the wind.
Aunty He's got one of my petunias, would you believe.
Stanley Shh.
Terry Will he do more magic?
Stanley Oh, don't suggest it.

The Unicorn stops running and offers Tracey the petunia

Tracey For me? Thank you. (*She kisses the Unicorn and sticks the flower in her hair*) You really are beautiful, very different from anything I've ever known, anyone I've ever known.

The Unicorn nuzzles her

Careful. You could blind someone with that. Just sit down and be quiet.

Tracey sits. The Unicorn lies beside her and whispers into her ear

Stanley He's whispering to her, cheeky monkey.
Aunty Can you hear?
Terry What?
Stanley No, you have to get really close to hear their voices.
Tracey Oh come on. There must be lots of pretty people in the Elysian Fields.
  Nymphs and shepherdesses and things like that.

The Unicorn shakes his head

There are in all the pictures I've seen.

The Unicorn whispers into Tracey's ear

Stanley He's telling lies.
Aunty Well, he's very attractive.
Stanley I thought I was attractive.
Terry I'm the one that's attractive.
Aunty All men are attractive, but not all men are unicorns.
Stanley I'm certainly not.
Aunty You're different.
Tracey I belong here, you see. I can't go dashing off past the moon, because
  I don't think people get back from there. It's sort of like heaven, isn't it?
  I mean it is heaven really.

The Unicorn nods his head

Yes. Well, you see, I quite like Peckham.
Stanley So do I.
Terry Do you?
Stanley There's people here, and ham suppers, garden sheds, shops.
Terry And Sharon.
Tracey Yes, I know there's not a lot of space, but when you come up here,
  and look over all the lights of the city, all those different people — —

The Unicorn puts his head in her lap

Oh, Arthur, I wish you were mine. I'd never want any other friends in all
the world. Will you be my friend forever?

The Unicorn looks up at the sky

No, I've told you. Here is where I live.

The Unicorn whispers into Tracey's ear

No, I don't prefer Harry.

The Unicorn whispers into Tracey's ear again

No, I'm not going to choose between you. Just enjoy being here on Telegraph Hill.

The Unicorn gets up and paces around

Arthur?
Aunty Oughtn't you to do something?
Stanley He might calm down if we leave him.
Aunty He might not.
Terry I've got this present.

The Unicorn turns towards Tracey and slowly advances on her lowering its head

Tracey Arthur, just settle down.

The Unicorn paws the ground

I'm not going away with you, and that's that.

The Unicorn moves closer to Tracey

Someone! Stanley!
Stanley Stop this nonsense at once!
Aunty At once, Arthur!

Stanley, Aunty Sharon and Terry come out of hiding and the Unicorn turns on them

Tracey What's the matter with him?
Stanley I think he wants to take you to the Elysian Fields, and I doubt if you'd enjoy it. It's mainly grass. Arthur, sit down, sit.
Terry On this, it's my present. (*He takes out another whoopee cushion*)
Aunty We don't want him making that sort of noise, for heaven's sake.

The Unicorn charges Stanley. Stanley sidesteps and puts his arm round the Unicorn's neck

Stanley Make him sit, go on make him sit!

The cast shout sit

Terry places the cushion at the Unicorn's rear end. The Unicorn sits and a pretty version of Vivaldi's "Four Seasons" is heard. The Unicorn calms and nods his head in time to the music.

Stanley There. Now behave and don't go frightening people.
Aunty Oh, that was brave, Terry, and very tasteful.
Terry I know a man, you see, did a swap with the other.
Stanley He didn't mean you any harm, love, but he might've done you harm sort of accidentally, kind of. That's the trouble with unicorns. They're very difficult, and this one's an only child. I think I'd better take him over here and have a word with him. Come along, Arthur. She's not cross with you, but she's not yours. Just learn to understand.

Stanley leads the Unicorn off

Tracey Don't hurt him. He's beautiful.
Aunty And Stanley, make sure you come back.
Terry (*to Tracey*) Are you all right, love? I've got an egg mayo sandwich here.
Aunty Where from?
Terry I made it myself. I'm not completely helpless, you know. (*He offers Tracey the paper bag*)
Tracey Thank you.
Aunty You've kept pretty quiet about your cooking.
Terry I'm not a fool, neither.

Stanley enters, with the Unicorn hand-puppet as described in Act I, Scene 8

Stanley Yes, well that's how it got to be. You must grow up and see sense.
Tracey Arthur!
Stanley He's come to say goodbye.
Tracey He's going away?
Stanley He has to, really, doesn't he? It's not an easy world for legendary creatures.
Tracey I suppose not. Goodbye, then, Arthur Unicorn. I won't forget you.
Aunty Goodbye, Arthur Unicorn. Has he got an egg to travel in?

Stanley takes an egg from his pocket

Stanley Yes. I'll just see him go and then be back to stay. Once you've shopped at Tesco's the Elysian Fields lose their attraction somehow.

Stanley exits

Aunty Home then, and a nice cup of camomile.

Aunty and Terry exit

Tracey (*looking up at the sky*) He'll soon be up there, going past the moon.

The buzzing sound of the egg taking off is heard

Goodbye.

Tracey exits

SCENE 7

The Jacksons' garden. Late evening

George enters limping. He is still wearing an eyepatch and has his horn growing on his forehead. He carries the row of petunias and a sack

George (*to the audience*) Everybody's left me on my own, and it's getting to be night time, and cold in the garden, and just watch this. (*Calling off*) Mother!

Mary enters dancing, holding her arms like a ballet dancer and humming a bit of Swan Lake

We haven't had any supper, Mother.
Mary I'm other worldly, now, George.
George Well, give us a cuddle and cook supper.
Mary I can't give you a cuddle because we'd scar each other if I did. And I'm beyond kitchen matters. (*She floats around and about*)

During the following Mary exits dancing and immediately returns without her unicorn horn

George (*to the audience*) You see? Nothing's going right. I don't want a new car, and swimming pool and barbecues if this is what's going to happen.

And the police have been in looking for the gold because they say I stole it — I've hidden it in this sack — and I want to kiss my wife, and I haven't got a job and I just want to be something ordinary again instead of something that's nothing. Mary, come back and talk to me. Look, we have to do something about this — (*He notices that Mary's horn has disappeared*) Where's your horn?

Mary Oh! It's gone! I feel quite bare without it, George.

George There's only one person who can take them away like that. The one who brought them in the first place, that dratted unicorn, doing his bits of magic. I wonder if something's happened to the one in here?

Mary They must've found him and persuaded him to change things.

George looks right into his sack, so that his head is completely hidden from view. During the following, unseen by the audience, he removes his Unicorn horn and eyepatch

Tracey, Terry, Aunty Sharon and Harry enter. Harry no longer has his horn growing from his forehead

Harry It's gone, Trace, so we can try to be an item, please, just as an experiment.

Tracey In time, Harry. Just leave it for the moment.

Mary Are we all going back to what we were?

George looks up out of his sack. He no longer has a unicorn horn growing on his forehead or his eyepatch

George No, we're not. I'm not going back to the bank, for one thing.

Harry Yours has gone, too, Dad.

George Exactly, I'm free. The weight of it was beginning to make my back ache. Where's Arthur?

Tracey Gone.

George Oh. Perhaps we could have been friends.

Aunty You hadn't the temperament and nor had he.

George Then I'll give up day dreaming and take up gardening.

Aunty Like me.

George Not quite like you, Aunty Sharon. I'll grow vegetables. Big juicy vegetables.

Aunty You'll need some flowers too, George.

Mary And I might take up ballet.

George Lovely.

Mary Is it Tracey?
Tracey Yes.
Mary Charmed to meet you, love.
Harry I might get to kiss her.
Tracey Possibly, I said possibly.
Terry What about us?
Aunty I think I'm happy with the three of us. Where's my Stanley?
Mary Oh, you and men, Aunty Sharon. What is it with you?
Aunty Oomph. And what's that?

The sound of the buzzing egg like an aeroplane is heard. It comes low and lands

Stanley (*off*) You've landed in the watering-can!
Harry Oh no, I don't want him back.
Tracey Not now we've said goodbye.
Mary He did things for me, though.
George He's got me fired, which I'm pleased about.
Stanley (*off*) Well, if you're sure you've changed, then, Arthur. All right.
Tracey Changed?
Stanley (*off*) Into a Shetland pony.

Everybody echoes Stanley's last sentence

Stanley enters. He has hand-puppet of a Shetland pony, operated like the Unicorn puppet

There are cries of "Ah!" amongst the cast

Stanley There! He changed himself to be close to me, really, and as I want to stay as part of all of you, I thought I'd become a milkman, and hope he grows big enough to pull me around.
Terry There aren't any milk carts anymore, but I know a man who does rides for kiddies in Margate.
George Well, there we are, it's a happy ending and it's getting late. Everyone had better stay the night.
Stanley And have a ham supper?
Terry I'll make it.
George And tomorrow, we can all have breakfast together, and there will be — —
All (*except George*) No!

George   There will be chocolates, because that's what's happened to
Auntie's golden horn. (*To the audience*)
                        And that's the story of the Unicorn,
                        Which ends quite happily, I'm glad to say,
                        So have a choc before you go away,
                        And think before you wish a dream come true,
                        Something like this might happen even to you.
                        And if it does, and seems to give you pain,
                        Remember to be like us, just change, and start again.

Music plays

Everybody dances and hands out chocolate from George's sack

THE END

FURNITURE AND PROPERTY LIST

Further dressing may be added at the director's discression.

ACT I

SCENE 1

On stage: Golden nosebag for **Stanley**

SCENE 2

On stage: nil

Off stage: Table laid for breakfast including four hard-boiled eggs, spoons
Four chairs
Parcel containing whoopee cushion (**George**)

SCENE 3

On stage: Four chairs on stage throughout

Off stage: Two computers (**Harry** and **Tracy**)

SCENE 4

On stage: No additional props required

Off stage: Lunch-box (**Aunty Sharon**)
Plastic container with a strip of petunias (**Aunty Sharon**)

SCENE 5

On stage: No additional props required

Personal: **George:** packet of sandwiches

SCENE 6

On stage:	No additional props required

Off stage: Table laid for breakfast including napkins, teapot, spoons, two normal hard-boiled eggs, two exploding hard-boiled eggs a darker colour — one containing a tiny figurine of Stanley, the other a tiny figurine of the Unicorn and a piece of paper (**Harry**)

Personal: **George**: Stanley glove puppet

SCENE 7

On stage: Two computers (**Tracey** and **Harry**)

SCENE 8

On stage: No additional props required

Off stage: Unicorn hand-puppet as described page 17 (**George**)

Personal: **George**: sandwich

SCENE 9

On stage: No additional props required

Off stage: Table laid for tea including Jaffa cakes, teacups, teapot and various other things.

Personal: **Unicorn**: two bouquets of flowers

ACT II

SCENE 1

On stage: Row of petunias
Four chairs on stage throughout. *On them*: whoopee cushion

Off stage: Trowel and small watering-can (**Aunty Sharon**)
Saw (**George**)

Furniture and Property List

On stage: No additional props required

Off stage: Table laid for breakfast including a breadknife, toast, marmalade
                    (**Stanley**)
                Tea-towel (**George**)
                Tea-towel (**Mary**)
                Bowl of cornflakes and mirror (**Harry**)
                Sticking-plaster (**Mary**)

On stage: Newspapers, etc. for **Tube Passengers**

Off stage: Golden unicorn horn (**George**)

Personal: **George**: eyepatch

On stage: No additional props required

Off stage: Two folders (**Harry** and **Tracey**)

On stage: No additional props required

On stage: nil

Off stage: Paper bag (**Terry**)
                Petunia (**Unicorn**)

Personal: **Terry**: whoopee cushion
                Stanley: egg

On stage: nil

Off stage: Sack containing chocolate (**George**)
                Hand-puppet of a Shetland pony (**Stanley**)

Personal: **Terry**: whoopee cushion
                Stanley: egg

LIGHTING PLOT

Practical fittings required: nil

Act I, SCENE 1

To open: General exterior lighting

No cues

Act I, SCENE 2

To open: Interior lighting; morning

No cues

Act I, SCENE 3

To open: Office interior lighting; morning

No cues

Act I, SCENE 4

To open: Exterior lighting; lunchtime

No cues

Act I, SCENE 5

To open: Office interior lighting; lunchtime

No cues

Act I, SCENE 6

To open: Interior lighting; morning

No cues

Lighting Plot

Act I, Scene 7

To open: Office interior lighting; morning

No cues

Act I, Scene 8

To open: Office interior lighting; morning

No cues

Act I, Scene 9

To open: Interior lighting; teatime

Cue 7   **George**: "I've got no job!"   (Page 25)
                   Black-out

Act II, Scene 1

To open: Exterior lighting; early evening

No cues

Act II, Scene 2

To open: Interior lighting; morning

No cues

Act II, Scene 3

To open: London tube train lighting, morning

No cues

Act II, Scene 4

To open: Exterior lighting; morning

No cues

Act II, Scene 5

To open: Interior lighting, morning

No cues

Act II, Scene 6

To open: Exterior lighting, evening

No cues

Act II, Scene 7

To open: Exterior lighting, late evening

No cues

EFFECTS PLOT

ACT I

Cue 1   **Aunty**:" ... back to bed."   (Page 4)
Front doorbell rings

Cue 2   **Aunty** sits on the cushion   (Page 5)
The cushion farts some of Vivaldi's "Four Seasons"

Cue 3   **Harry** and **Tracey** move to exit   (Page 8)
Faint buzzing noise

Cue 4   As Scene 4 begins   (Page 8)
Fade buzzing noise

Cue 5   **Aunty**: "Aah."   (Page 8)
Buzzing sound

Cue 6   **Terry**: " ... garden seat?"   (Page 9)
Buzzing sound fades

Cue 7   **Terry**: " ... when we're busy."   (Page 9)
Buzzing noise like a distant aeroplane

Cue 8   **Aunty**: "... around the city."   (Page 9)
Fade buzzing sound

Cue 9   **George**: " ... off their food."   (Page 10)
Buzzing noise like a distant aeroplane

Cue 10   **George**: " ... stomach buzz."   (Page 11)
Fade buzzing sound

Cue 11   **George**: " ... here at all!"   (Page 11)
Buzzing sound grows loud

Cue 12   **George** exits   (Page 11)
Buzzing sound dives then is silent

Cue 13   **Harry** hits one of the darker eggs   (Page 12)
The egg makes a loud metallic boing sound

Cue 28	**Female Passenger**: " ... us all."	(Page 37)
	Sound of tube train beginning to slow	
Cue 29	**George**: " ... stops to go."	(Page 38)
	Sound of tube train stopping, doors open	
Cue 30	**George**: " ... be a millionaire."	(Page 38)
	Tube train doors close and the train departs	
Cue 31	The **Unicorn** sits on the whoopee cushion	(Page 44)
	A pretty version of Vivaldi's "Four Seasons"	
Cue 32	**Tracey**: " ... going past the moon."	(Page 45)
	Buzzing sound	
Cue 33	**Aunty**: " ... what's that?"	(Page 47)
	Buzzing sound like an aeroplane. It comes low and lands	
Cue 34	**George**: " ... and start again."	(Page 48)
	Music plays	